Success With
Writing

■ SCHOLASTIC

Editor: Ourania Papacharalambous
Cover design by Tannaz Fassihi; cover illustration by Kevin Zimmer
Interior design by Michelle H. Kim
Interior illustrations by Mike Moran; © Shutterstock.com (14, 18)

ISBN 978-1-338-79874-6
Scholastic Inc., 557 Broadway, New York, NY 10012
Copyright © 2022 Scholastic Inc.
All rights reserved. Printed in the U.S.A.
First printing, January 2022
1 2 3 4 5 6 7 8 9 10   40 29 28 27 26 25 24 23 22

INTRODUCTION

One of the greatest challenges teachers and parents face is helping students develop independent writing skills. Each writing experience is unique and individualized. The high-interest topics and engaging exercises in *Scholastic Success With Writing* will both stimulate and encourage students as they develop their writing skills. On page 4, you will find a list of the key skills covered in the activities throughout this book. These grade-appropriate skills can be used in daily writing assignments such as journals, stories, and letters to help build confident, independent writers. Like a stepladder, this book will help students reach the next level of independent writing.

TABLE OF CONTENTS

Grade-Appropriate Skills Covered in
Scholastic Success With Writing: Grade 4

Write opinion pieces on topics or texts, supporting a point of view with reasons and information.

Introduce a topic or text clearly, state an opinion, and create an organizational structure in which related ideas are grouped to support the writer's purpose.

Provide reasons that are supported by facts and details.

Link opinion and reasons using words and phrases.

Provide a concluding statement or section related to the opinion presented.

Write informative/explanatory texts to examine a topic and convey ideas and information clearly.

Introduce a topic clearly and group related information in paragraphs and sections; include formatting, illustrations, and multimedia when useful to aiding comprehension.

Develop the topic with facts, definitions, concrete details, quotations, or other information and examples related to the topic.

Link ideas within categories of information using words and phrases.

Use precise language and domain-specific vocabulary to inform about or explain the topic.

Provide a concluding statement or section related to the information or explanation presented.

Write narratives to develop real or imagined experiences or events using effective technique, descriptive details, and clear event sequences.

Orient the reader by establishing a situation and introducing a narrator and/or characters; organize an event sequence that unfolds naturally.

Use dialogue and description to develop experiences and events or show the responses of characters to situations.

Use a variety of transitional words and phrases to manage the sequence of events.

Use concrete words and phrases and sensory details to convey experiences and events precisely.

Provide a conclusion that follows from the narrated experiences or events.

Demonstrate command of the conventions of standard English grammar and usage when writing or speaking.

Order adjectives within sentences according to conventional patterns.

Produce complete sentences, recognizing and correcting inappropriate fragments and run-ons.

Demonstrate command of the conventions of standard English capitalization, punctuation, and spelling when writing.

Use knowledge of language and its conventions when writing, speaking, reading, or listening.

Sassy Sentences

A **sentence** is a group of words that express a complete thought. If the sentence is complete, the meaning is clear. It contains a **subject** (the naming part) and a **predicate** (an action or state of being).

These are sentences:	These are not sentences:
Sally sells seashells by the seashore. Betty Botter bought a bit of better butter.	Pack of pickled peppers Flying up a flue

Make a complete sentence by adding a subject or a predicate to each partial sentence below. Try to create tongue twisters like the sentences above.

1 _____ flips fine flapjacks.

2 Sixty slippery seals _____.

3 _____ fed Ted _____.

4 Ruby Rugby's baby brother _____.

5 _____ manages an imaginary magazine.

6 Sam's sandwich shop _____.

7 _____ back blue balloons.

8 _____ pink peacock pompously _____.

9 Pete's father Pete _____.

10 _____ sawed Mr. Saw's _____.

11 A flea and a fly _____.

12 _____ black-backed bumblebee.

Link It Together

A sentence needs two parts, a subject and a predicate, to express a complete thought.
The **subject part** tells whom or what the sentence is about. The **predicate part** tells what the
subject is or does.

One picture   _is worth a thousand words._

  subject part   **predicate part**

Birds of a feather   _flock together._

  subject part   **predicate part**

**Read the subject and predicate parts from some other famous sayings.
Write _S_ next to each subject part. Write _P_ next to each predicate part.**

_____ must go on

_____ spoils the whole barrel

_____ the show

_____ every cloud

_____ catches the worm

_____ the early bird

_____ gathers no moss

_____ has a silver lining

_____ makes waste

_____ one rotten apple

_____ a rolling stone

_____ haste

Now combine the subject and predicate parts to create these famous sayings.

1 _____

2 _____

3 _____

4 _____

5 _____

6 _____

That's Groovy!

There are four kinds of sentences. Each one does something different.

A **declarative sentence** tells something. It is a **statement** and ends with a period.

My grandparents grew up during the 1960s.

An **interrogative sentence** asks something. It is a **question** and ends with a question mark.

Do you know who the hippies were?

An **imperative sentence** tells someone to do something. It is a **command** and ends with a period.

Check out this photo of my grandmother.

An **exclamatory sentence** shows strong feeling. It is an **exclamation** and ends with an exclamation mark.

Now, that's one strange-looking outfit she has on!

**Read the following sentences. Identify what kind of sentence each one is.
Write *S* for statement, *Q* for question, *C* for command, and *E* for exclamation.**

_____ 1 Grandma says that fashion changed slightly in the 1970s.

_____ 2 What an amazing time it must have been!

_____ 3 Here's a photo of my grandfather in his twenties.

_____ 4 How do you like those sideburns and the long hair?

_____ 5 Take a look at what he's wearing.

_____ 6 I don't believe those bell-bottoms and sandals!

_____ 7 Please tell me he doesn't have long hair.

_____ 8 I'm glad these fashions are no longer in style!

_____ 9 One day our grandchildren may laugh at us.

_____ 10 What's so funny about what we're wearing?

Now, look at the "photos" below and write a statement (S), a question (Q), a command (C), and an exclamation (E) about each one. Make sure to begin and end your sentences correctly.

S _____

Q _____

C _____

E _____

S _____

Q _____

C _____

E _____

☆ Invite someone to listen as you expressively read aloud your sentences. Show what kind of sentences they are by the way that you read them.

A Whale of a Fish

When you write, the words and phrases in your sentences must be in an order that makes sense. Compare the sentences in each pair. Which ones make more sense?

An enormous fish what the whale shark is!
What an enormous fish the whale shark is!

The largest fish in the world the whale shark is.
The whale shark is the largest fish in the world.

Use each group of words to write a sentence that makes sense.

1 of 60 feet? that the whale shark Did you know to a length can grow

_____

2 are not a threat These huge creatures like some other sharks are. to humans

_____

3 to look for float near the surface plankton and tiny fish. Whale sharks

_____

Rewrite the sentences below in an order that makes better sense.

1 An estimated 32,000 known species of fish there are in the world.

_____

2 Of all these species one of the smallest is the dwarf pygmy goby?

_____

3 When it is fully grown is less than a half-inch long this species of goby!

_____

Number Sentences

Words such as *who, what, where, why, when,* and *how,* and helping verbs such as *is, are, was, were, do, did,* and *can* at the beginning of sentences signal interrogative sentences or questions. Read the examples below.

> **What** *is an odd number?*
> **Are** *odd numbers divisible by 2?*
>
> **Do** *you know what an even number is?*
> **Is** *2 an odd number or an even number?*

Change each statement below into a question. Remember to begin and end each sentence correctly.

1. Numbers that cannot be divided evenly by 2 are called odd numbers.

   _____

2. All even numbers can be divided evenly by 2.

   _____

3. Zero is considered an even number.

   _____

4. Numbers that have 0, 2, 4, 6, or 8 in the ones place are even numbers.

   _____

5. Odd numbers end in 1, 3, 5, 7, or 9.

   _____

6. The number 317,592 is an even number because it ends in 2.

   _____

7. The sum is always an even number when you add two even numbers.

   _____

Proofing Pays

Capitalization and end punctuation help show where one sentence ends and the next one begins. Whenever you write, proofread to make sure each sentence begins with a capital letter and ends correctly. Here's an example of how to mark the letters that should be capitalized.

> have you ever heard of a Goliath birdeater? it is the world's largest spider. this giant tarantula can grow to 11 inches in length and weigh about 6 ounces. now that's a big spider! although it is called a birdeater, it usually eats earthworms. occasionally it will also eat small insects. these spiders are mostly found in rain forests.

Read the passage below. It is about another amazing animal, but it is not so easy to read because the writer forgot to add end punctuation and use capital letters at the beginning of sentences. Proofread the passage. Mark the letters that should be capitals with the capital letter symbol. Put the correct punctuation marks at the ends of sentences. Then, reread the passage.

think about the fastest car you've ever seen in the Indianapolis 500 race that's about

how fast peregrine falcons dive   they can actually reach speeds of over 200 miles an hour

while diving   how incredibly fast they are   peregrine falcons are also very powerful birds

did you know that they can catch and kill their prey in the air using their sharp claws

what's really amazing is that peregrine falcons live in both the country and the city   keep

on the lookout if you're ever in New York City   believe it or not, it is home to several falcons

Spout Some Specifics

To be a good writer, it is important to know what you are writing about, to be specific, and to include details. All this helps create a picture for your readers and will make your writing more interesting and informative. Compare the two phrases below. Which one is more specific, interesting, and informative? Which one creates a more vivid picture?

a vehicle **or** *an old, rusty, dilapidated pickup truck with flat tires*

For each general word or phrase, write a more specific word. Add details to describe each specific word.

		Specific Word	**Details**
1	a body of water		
2	a piece of furniture		
3	an article of clothing		
4	a child's toy		
5	a noise or sound		
6	a tool		
7	a group of people		
8	a reptile		
9	garden plants		
10	a kind of fruit		

Make It Interesting

A sentence can be very simple. This sentence tells who did what:

The crew worked.

As you write and revise your writing, add details about people, places, or things, or about where, when, and what happens. This will make your writing more interesting. Here's how the sentence above was revised several times. Each sentence gives a little more information.

The construction crew worked.

The construction crew worked quickly.

The construction crew worked quickly to clear the rubble.

The construction crew worked quickly to clear the rubble at the building site.

The construction crew worked quickly yesterday to clear the rubble at the building site.

Rewrite the sentences below each picture three times. Add new details in each sentence.

The children played.

A package arrived.

1 _____

_____

2 _____

_____

3 _____

_____

_____

1 _____

_____

2 _____

_____

3 _____

_____

_____

Order the Combination

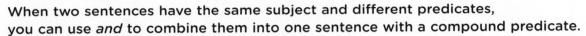

When two sentences have different subjects and the same predicate,
you can use the conjunction *and* to combine them into one sentence
with a compound subject.

My friends ordered a pepperoni pizza. I ordered a pepperoni pizza.

My friends and I ordered a pepperoni pizza.

When two sentences have the same subject and different predicates,
you can use *and* to combine them into one sentence with a compound predicate.

My mom ordered. She chose pasta.

My mom ordered and chose pasta.

When two sentences have the same subject and predicate and different objects, you can
combine them into one sentence with a compound object using *and*.

My dad wanted anchovies on his pizza. He also wanted onions.

My dad wanted anchovies and onions on his pizza.

**Fill in the missing subject, object, or predicate in each set of sentences. Then,
combine the sentences by making compound subjects, objects, or predicates
using *and*.**

1 _____ are sweet and juicy.

_____ are sweet and juicy.

_____

2 The farmer _____ beans.

He _____ beans, too.

_____

3 I like _____ more than broccoli or cauliflower.

I like _____ more than broccoli or cauliflower.

_____

A New Challenge

You can show how two ideas are related by combining two simple sentences. To combine sentences, you need a comma and the conjunctions *and*, *but*, or *or*. *And* shows a link between the ideas, *but* shows a contrast, and *or* shows a choice. The new sentence is called a compound sentence.

My sister wants to join a football team. My parents aren't so happy about it.

My sister wants to join a football team, **but** *my parents aren't so happy about it.*

Annie is determined. Her friends think she'd make a great place kicker.

Annie is determined, **and** *her friends think she'd make a great place kicker.*

Should Annie play football? Should she try something else?

Should Annie play football, **or** *should she try something else?*

Combine each pair of sentences. Use *and, but,* or *or* to show the connection between the ideas and make a compound sentence.

1 My sister Annie has always participated in sports. Many say she's a natural athlete.

_____

_____

_____

2 Soccer, basketball, and softball are fun. She wanted a new challenge.

_____

_____

_____

3 Will Dad convince her to try skiing? Will he suggest ice skating?

_____

_____

_____

Hot Subjects

If two sentences share the same subject, information about the subject can be written as a phrase after the subject in the new sentence. Be sure to use commas to set apart the phrase from the rest of the sentence.

Sentence 1: *The Gateway Arch is America's tallest human-made monument.*
Sentence 2: *The monument rises 630 feet above the ground.*
Combined: *The Gateway Arch, America's tallest human-made monument, rises 630 feet above the ground.*

Read the sentences. Combine the ideas in each pair into one sentence by including information in a phrase after the subject in the sentence.

1. The Caspian Sea is the world's largest lake.
   The lake covers an area about the same size as Montana.

   _____

   _____

2. The Komodo dragon is a member of the monitor family.
   It can grow to a length of 10 feet.

   _____

   _____

3. Our closest star is the sun.
   It is estimated to be more than 27,000,000°F at its core.

   _____

   _____

Sentence Building

When you write about something, try to include interesting details. Sometimes you can take the important details from several related sentences and add them to the main sentence.

> *Kyle and Jim had a great plan.*
> *They're my brothers.*
> *The plan was for a tree house.*

Now here's a sentence that combines all the important details.

> *My brothers Kyle and Jim had a great plan for a tree house.*

Read each group of sentences. Take the important details from the two related sentences and add them to the main sentence to make one sentence.

1 My brothers built a tree house. They built it in the old oak tree. It's in our backyard.

_____

_____

2 Jim made a ladder for the tree house. He made it out of rope. It is sturdy.

_____

_____

3 Kyle bought paint. The paint was brown. He bought a gallon.

_____

_____

4 Kyle and Jim finished painting. They painted the walls. It took an hour.

_____

Applause for the Clause

Sometimes you can use words such as *when, because, while,* and *before* to combine two sentences with related ideas into one sentence that has a main clause and a dependent clause.

A **clause** is a group of words with a subject and a verb. An **independent clause** can stand alone as a sentence, or be joined to another independent clause. A **dependent clause** cannot stand alone.

> *Lee woke up late today. He realized he hadn't set his alarm last night.*
> <u>When Lee woke up late today,</u> <u>he realized he hadn't set his alarm last night.</u>
>   ↑   ↑
> This is a **dependent clause**.   This is an **independent clause**.

Add a comma after the dependent clause if it comes before the main clause. If the dependent clause follows the main clause, you do not need a comma.

> *Because he was going to be late for school, Lee was upset.*
> *Lee was upset because he was going to be late for school.*

Use the word inside the parentheses to combine each pair of sentences into one.

1 The movie was over. The power went out. (before)

_____

_____

2 Jago was in his room. He had homework to do. (because)

_____

_____

3 I waited for my parents to come home. I watched a movie. (while)

_____

_____

Triple the Fun

When you write, you may want to list three or more items or ideas in a series in a single sentence. Be sure to use a comma after each item in a series except after the last item.

Max dressed quickly, ate breakfast, and raced out the door.
Luis, Jamie, Leroy, and Sam met Max at the baseball field.
They were hopeful, excited, and nervous about their first game.

**Answer each question below in a complete
sentence. Use commas where they are needed.
Make sure each sentence begins and ends correctly.**

1 What are the titles of three books you've read recently or would like to read?

_____

_____

2 What are four of the planets in our solar system that are closer to the sun than Neptune?

_____

_____

3 What are three green leafy vegetables? _____

_____

4 What countries would you like to visit? Include at least three in your answer.

_____

_____

5 What are three months that fall between January and July? _____

_____

_____

Comma Capers

You know that you must use commas in a series of three or more items.

Max, Sam, and Alex ordered burgers, fries, and milkshakes for lunch.

Here are some additional rules you need to know about commas. Use commas:
- to set off the name of the person or group you are addressing

Here's your order, boys.

- after words like *yes*, *no*, and *well*

Well, what do you want to do now?

- before a conjunction that joins two sentences

The boys finished lunch, and then they went to a movie.

Read the sentences below. Decide which ones need commas and which ones do not. Use this symbol $\wedge$ to show where commas belong.

1   I'd like a bike a pair of in-line skates and a snowboard for my birthday.

2   Well my friend you can't always have what you want when you want it.

3   No but I can always hope!

4   I used to like skateboarding but now I prefer snowboarding and ice skating.

5   What sports games or hobbies do you enjoy most Jody?

6   I learned to ski last year and now I'm taking ice-skating lessons.

Review the four rules above for using commas. Then, write an original sentence for each rule. Begin and end each sentence correctly. Remember to check your spelling.

1   _____

2   _____

3   _____

4   _____

Show Time

Sometimes a writer can change the order of the words in a sentence to make it more interesting.

Gina's phone rang just as the girls were about to leave.

Just as the girls were about to leave, Gina's phone rang.

Do not forget to add a comma when you begin a sentence with a clause or a phrase that cannot stand alone, as in the second sentence above.

Rewrite each sentence by changing the order of the words.

1 Marta opened the front door while Gina answered the phone. _____

_____

_____

2 The caller hung up just as Gina said, "Hello." _____

_____

_____

3 The girls were going to miss the one o'clock show unless they hurried.

_____

_____

4 The bus had already come and gone by the time they got to the corner.

_____

_____

5 The next bus to town finally showed up after the girls had waited a half hour.

_____

_____

It Keeps on Going

Writers sometimes make the mistake of running together two or more sentences without telling how the ideas are related. This kind of sentence is called a **run-on sentence.**

Today was the best day ever we checked into our hotel at the beach my sister and I were so excited we could see the giant waves from the room.

To fix a run-on sentence, identify each complete thought and break it into shorter sentences.

Today was the best day ever! We checked into our hotel at the beach. My sister and I were so excited. We could see the giant waves from the room!

Rewrite each run-on sentence correctly. Use correct capitalization and punctuation.

1 The United States is the top meat-eating country in the world each person consumes about 220 pounds of meat each year beef is the most commonly eaten meat.

_____

_____

_____

2 Have you ever noticed that Abraham Lincoln faces right on a penny he is not the only president on a U.S. coin who does Thomas Jefferson faces right on newer nickels too?

_____

_____

_____

3 It would be fantastic to have a robot to do all my chores, help do my homework, and play games I really think the day will come unfortunately, it won't come soon enough for me.

_____

_____

_____

A Long School Year

Have you ever accidentally left out words when you write? Whenever you write, it is always a good idea to proofread for words that may be missing. Here is an example of what to do when you want to add a missing word as you proofread.

>   email
> I got an ∧ from my friend last night.
>   met
> We ∧ last summer when my family was in Japan.

Read the passage below about school in Japan. Twenty-one words are missing. Figure out what they are and add them to the sentences. Use the ∧ symbol to show where each missing word belongs. Then, write each missing word above the sentence. Hint: Every sentence has at least one missing word.

How would like to go to school on Saturdays? If you lived in the of Japan, that's just

where you could be each Saturday morning. I have a who lives in Japan. Yuichi explained

that attend classes five and one-half a week. The day is on Saturday. I was also surprised

to that the Japanese school is one of the longest in the world—about 220 days. It begins in

the of April. While we have over two months off each, students in Japan get their in late July

and August. School then again in fall and ends in March. The people of believe that a

good is very important. Children are required to attend school from the age of six to the of

fifteen. They have elementary and middle just like we do. Then most go on to high for

another three years. Yuichi says that students work very because the standards are so high.

He and some of his friends even extra classes after school. They all want to get into a

good someday.

Parts of a Paragraph

A **paragraph** is a group of sentences that tells about one main idea. The **topic sentence** tells the main idea and is usually the first sentence. **Supporting sentences** tell more about the main idea. The **closing sentence** of a paragraph often retells the main idea in a different way. Here are the parts for one paragraph.

Paragraph Title: Starting Over

Topic Sentence: Today started off badly and only got worse.

Supporting Sentences:
1. Everyone in my family woke up late this morning.
2. I had only 15 minutes to get ready and catch the bus.
3. I dressed as fast as I could, grabbed an apple and my backpack, and raced to get to the bus stop on time.
4. Fortunately, I just made it.
5. Unfortunately, the bus was pulling away when several kids pointed out that I had on two different shoes.

Closing Sentence: At that moment, I wanted to start the day over.

When you write a paragraph, remember these rules:
- **Indent** the first line to let readers know that you are beginning a paragraph.
- **Capitalize** the first word of each sentence.
- **Punctuate** each sentence correctly (? ! . ,).

Use all the information above to write the paragraph. Be sure to follow the rules.

_____
paragraph title

_____

_____

_____

_____

_____

_____

What's the Topic?

A topic sentence tells the main idea of the paragraph.
It usually answers several of these questions:

| Who? | What? | Where? | When? | Why? | How? |

Here are some examples.

The doe and her fawn faced many dangers in the forest.
We were amazed by our guest's rude behavior.
Baking bread from scratch is really not so difficult, or so I thought.
Getting up in the morning is the hardest thing to do.

Did these topic sentences grab your attention? A good topic sentence should.

Here are some topics. Write a topic sentence for each one.

1 convincing someone to try octopus soup

_____

_____

2 an important person in your life

_____

_____

3 an embarrassing moment

_____

_____

4 the importance of Independence Day

_____

_____

Topic Talk

Most paragraphs begin with a topic sentence, but it can appear elsewhere in a paragraph. Sometimes a topic sentence is located at the end of a paragraph or even in the middle.

> *A boiling mass of clouds was almost overhead. A bolt of lightning streaked across the darkened sky. Thunder boomed, and it began to rain and hail. We had to find a safe place quickly! There wasn't a moment to spare because early summer storms sometimes turn into tornadoes.*

In the paragraph above, the topic sentence is located at the end of the paragraph. Read the paragraph again. This time, try the topic sentence elsewhere in the paragraph.

Each paragraph below is missing a topic sentence. Think about the supporting sentences. What main idea do you think they support? Write a topic sentence to tell the main idea of each paragraph.

1 The days are growing longer. The winter snows are melting as the temperatures rise. Colorful crocuses are popping up here and there. Robins have begun to return north,

and creatures are beginning to come out of their winter burrows. _____

_____

2 The last weekend in June is quickly approaching. You know what that means.

_____

_____

This year the festivities will begin at 10:00 A.M. at Twin Lakes Picnic Grove, pavilion 12. As always, there will be music, dancing, lots of great food, games, and some new surprises! We look forward to seeing you.

3 _____

It was fun and easy. Students, parents, and teachers began saving the box tops from all Healthful Foods products. After we collected 100,000 box tops, we mailed them to Healthful Foods headquarters. We earned 10 cents for each box top for a total of $10,000. Our school will use the money to buy more computers.

A Lot of Details

When you are ready to write a topic sentence, think about the main topic or idea of the paragraph you will be writing and the details you plan to include. Then, jot down several possible sentences and choose the best one. Remember that a topic sentence can answer several questions: *Who? What? Where? When? Why? How?*

Tony Hawk
- skateboarder   - turned professional at age 14
- retired   - made history at Summer X Games in 1999—landed a "900" (a complete somersault done 2 ½ times in midair)

Possible topic sentences: *There is no other skateboarder like Tony Hawk.*
Tony Hawk was an extraordinary skateboarder.
Tony Hawk is a legend in skateboarding.

Read topics with details. Write two topic sentences for each subject below.

1 **Pet Rocks**	2 **Komodo Dragon**	3 **A Great Dessert**
— fad in the 1970s	— member of monitor family	— slice a banana
— idea came from Gary Dahl, a salesman	— grows to 10 feet and weighs 300 pounds	— add vanilla ice cream
— sold rocks as pets	— meat eater	— sprinkle on some walnuts
— came with a manual	— dangerous to humans	— cover with lots of hot fudge sauce
— manual had tips on how to teach a pet rock tricks	— largest lizard in the world	— top with mounds of whipped cream and a cherry
	— long neck and tail	
	— found on Komodo Island	

1 _____

_____

2 _____

_____

3 _____

_____

Remember that the supporting sentences you write support or tell more about the main idea in your topic sentence. Read the paragraph below. Draw one line under the topic sentence. Draw two lines under the supporting sentences. Check (√) the closing sentence.

Tony Hawk

Tony Hawk was an extraordinary skateboarder. He turned professional when he was only 14 years old. Now retired, Tony made history in 1999 by landing a trick called the "900" at the Summer X Games. Tony Hawk may just be the greatest skateboarder ever.

Review the topics on the previous page. Choose one. Then, review the details listed about the topic you chose. Next, use the information to write a topic sentence and at least three supporting sentences. Include a closing sentence and a title. Write the paragraph below.

_____

_____

_____

_____

_____

_____

_____

Make a list of topics you would like to write about. Choose one. On another sheet of paper, list details you know about the topic. Do some research, if necessary. Then, write a topic sentence and several supporting sentences.

Drizzle With Details

A good paragraph needs supporting sentences that tell more about the main idea of the topic sentence. Supporting sentences are sometimes called detail sentences. Every detail sentence in a paragraph must relate to the main idea. In the following paragraph, the one supporting sentence that does not relate to the main idea has been underlined.

My first day of softball practice was a total disaster! Not only was I ten minutes late, but I also forgot my glove. Then, during batting practice, I missed the ball every time I took a swing. I definitely have improved on my catching skills. To make matters even worse, I tripped in the outfield and twisted my ankle. I was definitely not off to a very good start.

Read the following paragraph. Underline the topic sentence. Then, cross out any supporting sentences that do not relate to the main idea.

Yesterday our science class went on a field trip to a pond. Next month, we're going to the ocean. That will be fun. We've been studying the pond as an ecosystem in class. Our teacher wanted us to observe firsthand all the different habitats in and around the pond. She had us keep a checklist of the different kinds of plants and animals in each pond habitat. One of the boys accidentally fell in. He was really embarrassed. Along the water's edge, I saw several kinds of plants partly underwater, two salamanders, snails, and water bugs. I observed many different habitats.

**Read the title and topic sentence for each of the following paragraph plans.
Write four supporting sentences that relate to and support each one.**

1 Paragraph Title: Uniforms—To Wear or Not to Wear?
Topic Sentence: *Our school should require all students to wear uniforms.*

   1. _____

   2. _____

   3. _____

   4. _____

2 Paragraph Title: An Adventure in Dreamland
Topic Sentence: *Last night, I had the most incredible dream.*

   1. _____

   2. _____

   3. _____

   4. _____

3 Paragraph Title: A Great Day
Topic Sentence: *I will always remember this day as the best of my life.*

   1. _____

   2. _____

   3. _____

   4. _____

A Musical Lesson

There are many kinds of paragraphs. When you write a **comparison paragraph**, you compare by telling how things are similar and contrast by telling how things are different. You can use a Venn diagram to help organize your ideas. Here is an example.

Trumpet   **Both**   **Violin**

- brass
- has a mouthpiece
- has three valves

- are played in orchestras
- musical instruments
- take practice

- wood
- four strings
- played with a bow

Complete the paragraph using details to compare and contrast the trumpet and violin.

Trumpet Versus Violin

The trumpet and violin are both musical instruments that are _____

_____. However, there are

some important differences. The trumpet _____

_____

_____

On the other hand, the violin _____

_____

_____

Both instruments _____

_____

_____

Is That a Fact?

What is the difference between a fact and an opinion? A **fact** can be checked or proven. An **opinion** is what someone believes or feels about something. An opinion cannot be proven.

Read each sentence. Write *F* next to each fact. Write *O* next to each opinion.

_____ **1** Everyone in the world thinks chocolate makes the best candy.

_____ **2** In Switzerland, the average person eats about 19 pounds of chocolate in a year.

_____ **3** That means the Swiss eat about 164 million pounds of chocolate annually.

_____ **4** I think Americans eat more chocolate than that.

_____ **5** People also use chocolate to make drinks and to flavor recipes.

_____ **6** There's nothing better than a chocolate doughnut with chocolate glaze.

Look at the pictures. Write one fact and one opinion about each snack food. Use clue words such as *think, best, believe, like,* and *dislike* to signal an opinion.

1 Fact: _____

_____

Opinion: _____

_____

2 Fact: _____

_____

Opinion: _____

_____

I'm Convinced!

In a **persuasive paragraph**, you give an opinion about something and try to convince readers to think or feel the way you do. A convincing persuasive paragraph includes:

- a topic sentence that clearly states your opinion
- a closing sentence that summarizes your opinion
- reasons that support your opinion
- facts to back up your opinion

Pretend you are a world-famous chef who prepares dishes that include edible insects—insects that you can eat. You want to persuade people to include insects in their diet. Here is a topic sentence for a persuasive paragraph: *Everyone should try cooking with insects.*

Here are some reasons and facts.

- **Insects such as mealworms, crickets, and weevils are edible.**
- **People in many cultures around the world eat insects.**
- **Many insects are low in fat and rich in vitamins.**
- **Insects are really quite delicious.**

Now put it all together. Write a persuasive paragraph that includes a title and a strong closing sentence. Remember the rules for writing a paragraph.

Paragraph Title: _____

Topic Sentence: _____

_____

Reasons/Facts: _____

_____

_____

_____

_____

Closing Sentence: _____

_____

Step by Step

When you write an **expository paragraph**, you give facts and information, explain ideas, or give directions. It can also include opinions. Here are some topic ideas for an expository paragraph:

Explain how to play the flute.

Tell what skills you need to skateboard.

Explain how to bathe a dog.

Give the facts about your favorite band.

Here is an example of an expository paragraph. It explains how to fry an egg.

Frying an egg is not that difficult. After melting a bit of butter in a frying pan, just crack the eggshell along the rim of the pan and let the egg drop into the pan. Do it gently so the yolk does not break. Let the egg fry over low heat for about a minute or so. That is all it takes.

Complete the following topics for expository paragraphs with your own ideas.

Explain how to	Give facts about	Tell why
_____	_____	_____
_____	_____	_____

Use the form below to develop one of your ideas for an expository paragraph. Then, use the plan to write your paragraph on another sheet of paper.

Paragraph Title: _____

Topic Sentence: _____

_____

Details/Facts/Steps: _____

_____

_____

_____

Closing Sentence: _____

_____

A Sentence Relationship

A **cause** is the reason something happens. An **effect** is the result of the cause, or what actually happens. Words such as *so*, *because*, and *since* are used in cause-and-effect sentences.

effect   cause
School was canceled today **because** *the storm dumped two feet of snow.*

cause   effect
Since *there was no school today, I went back to bed and slept another hour.*

Add a cause to each sentence about the day school was canceled because of snow.

1 _____

_____ many shops, stores, and offices were closed.

2 My friends and I love snow days _____

_____.

3 _____

_____ it took several minutes to open the back door.

4 Our snow blower would not start _____

_____.

Add an effect to each of the following sentences.

1 I shoveled snow for two hours, _____

_____.

2 My sister could not find her boots, _____

_____.

3 _____

_____ since our street wasn't plowed until noon.

What a Mess!

You can write a paragraph using a cause-and-effect relationship. One way to begin is to state a cause. Then, you write about the effects that happen as a result of that cause.

> *The piercing sound of the smoke alarm reminded Max that he had forgotten to check the pot of stew heating up on the stove. The stew had boiled over, the bottom of the pot was scorched, and smoke was filling the kitchen. Dinner was obviously ruined, and Max was in big trouble. What a mess!*

Answer each question about the paragraph above.

1 What was the cause? _____

_____

2 What were the effects? List them. _____

_____

Read the first sentence of the following paragraph. It states a cause. What might happen as a result? Continue the paragraph. Write what you think the effects will be.

I walked into my room just as Sebastian, our very inquisitive cat, managed to tip over

the goldfish bowl that had been on my desk. _____

_____

_____

_____

_____

_____

A Vivid Picture

A **descriptive paragraph** creates a vivid image or picture for readers. By choosing just the right adjectives, you can reveal how something looks, sounds, smells, tastes, or feels. Compare the sentences below. Which one creates a more vivid picture?

The pizza with sausage and onions tasted so good.

The smooth, sweet sauce and bubbly mozzarella topped with chunks of extra hot sausage and thin slivers of sweet onion on a perfectly baked, thin crust delighted my taste buds.

Cut out a picture of something interesting and paste it in the box. Then, brainstorm a list adjectives and descriptive phrases to tell about it.

Now, write a paragraph about the picture. Begin your paragraph with a topic sentence that will grab readers. Add supporting sentences that include the adjectives and descriptive phrases you listed to create a vivid picture.

Numerous, Spectacular Words

When you write, do you sometimes overuse descriptive words like *good, bad, nice,* or *wonderful*? Overused words can make your writing boring.

> *The weather was good for our first camping trip. (spectacular)*
> *A ranger gave us some really good tips about the park. (useful)*
> *My older brother is a good fly fisherman. (skilled)*
> *He said his equipment is too good for me to use, though! (valuable)*

Reread the sentences, but this time replace *good* with the word in parentheses, or you can use a thesaurus to help find synonyms.

Identify six overused words in the passage. List them below. Then, use a thesaurus to find three synonyms for each. List these to the right. Choose one for each overused word. Cross out the overused words in the passage and write the more effective synonym above it.

Our family has a dog named Scooter. He's normally very good, until it's time to bathe him. That's when our nice, little terrier turns into a big, furry monster. Scooter isn't really bad. He's just hard to handle when he doesn't want to do something. I think he's afraid of water. You should see how sad he looks once we manage to get him into the tub.

1 _____ _____

2 _____ _____

3 _____ _____

4 _____ _____

5 _____ _____

6 _____ _____

Action Alert

Think about the verbs that you choose to express action in your sentences. Are they as exact as they can be? Exact verbs create a more precise picture of what happened.

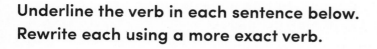 The child <u>broke</u> the plastic toy.
The child <u>smashed</u> the plastic toy.
The child <u>cracked</u> the plastic toy.

Underline the verb in each sentence below. Rewrite each using a more exact verb.

1 Three young hikers went up the steep hill.

_____

2 A lone runner ran around the track.

_____

3 The wind blew through the treetops.

_____

4 The janitor cleaned the scuff marks off the floor.

_____

5 The audience laughed at the hilarious scene.

_____

6 The diners ate the delicious meal.

_____

7 The young tourists liked the castle most of all.

_____

Colorful Clues

You can compare two things that are not alike in order to give your readers a clearer and more colorful picture. When you use *like* or *as* to make a comparison, it is called a **simile**.

> *Max is **as** slow **as** molasses when he doesn't want to do something.*
> *My sister leaped over the puddles **like** a frog to avoid getting her shoes wet.*

When you make a comparison without *like* or *as*, it is called a **metaphor**. You compare things directly, saying the subject is something else.

> *The disturbed anthill was a whirlwind of activity.*
> *Jenny and I were all ears as we listened to the latest gossip.*

Finish the metaphors and similes.

1 Crowds of commuters piled into the subway cars like _____

_____.

2 Chirping crickets on a warm summer night are _____

_____.

3 After rolling in the mud, our dog looked like _____

4 Happiness is _____.

5 Just learning to walk, the toddler was as wobbly as _____

_____.

6 After scoring the winning point, I felt as _____

_____.

7 Having a tooth filled is about as much fun as _____

_____.

Adding Spice

Sometimes you can spice up your writing by giving human characteristics and qualities to non-human things, such as animals and objects. This is called **personification**.

The sagging roof groaned under the weight of all the snow.

The falling leaves danced in the wind.

You can also use **hyperbole**, or deliberate exaggeration, to make a point clearer or to add drama to your writing.

The lost hiker is so hungry he could eat a bear.

Yesterday was so hot, we could have fried eggs on the sidewalk.

Personify the animal or object in each sentence by giving it human qualities.

1. The rusted hinges on the old wooden door _____

_____.

2. As several birds began feasting on the farmer's corn, the scarecrow _____

_____.

3. A gentle summer breeze _____

_____.

Complete each sentence with an example of a hyperbole.

1. The salsa was so spicy _____

_____.

2. The pumpkin grew so large _____

_____.

3. My room was so cold last night that by morning _____

_____.

Story Time

A story has **characters**, a **setting** (where and when the story takes place), and a **plot** (the events that happen in a story). The main character often faces a problem that is introduced at the **beginning** of the story, developed in the **middle**, and solved at the **end**.

Think about a story you would like to write. Answer the questions below to develop your story. Then, write your story on another sheet of paper.

1 What or who is the story about? _____

_____

_____

2 Where and when does it take place? _____

_____

_____

3 How will the story begin? _____

_____

_____

4 What happens in the middle? _____

_____

_____

5 How will the story end? _____

_____

_____

_____

What Did You Say?

Some stories may include **dialogue**, or the exact words of story characters. Dialogue lets readers know something about the characters, plot, setting, and problem or conflict in a story. Use quotation marks around a speaker's exact words and commas to set off quotations. Remember to put periods, question marks, exclamation points, and commas inside the quotation marks.

"Get away from my bowl!" yelled Little Miss Muffet when she saw the spider.

"Please don't get so excited," replied the startled spider. "I just wanted a little taste. I've never tried curds and whey before!"

Complete the dialogue between the fairy tale or nursery rhyme characters. Include quotation marks and commas where they belong and the correct end punctuation.

1 When Baby Bear saw the strange girl asleep in his bed, he asked his parents, _____

_____

His mother replied, _____

2 When Jack realized he was about to fall down the hill with a pail of water, he yelled,

_____

_____

_____ cried Jill, as she went tumbling down the hill after Jack.

3 Humpty Dumpty was sitting on the wall when he suddenly fell off. On the way down

he shouted, _____

Two of the king's men approached. One whispered nervously

to the other, _____

_____

Let's Get Organized

When you write a report or story, it helps to review your notes and organize them into an outline to show the order in which you want to discuss them.

Chester Greenwood ⟶ subject of the report

I. **Who was Chester Greenwood?** ⟶ main idea becomes topic sentence
   A. born in 1858 ⟶ supporting details become supporting sentences
   B. grew up in Farmington, Maine
   C. as a child had ear problems in winter

II. **His first invention: earmuffs**
   A. needed a way to protect ears from cold
   B. 1873 at age 15 began testing his ideas
   C. idea for fur-covered earflaps worked
   D. people saw and also wanted earflaps

III. **His later accomplishments**
   A. founded a telephone company
   B. manufactured steam heaters
   C. over 100 inventions

Use the outline above to answer the questions.

1 What is the topic of the report? _____

_____

2 How many paragraphs will there be? _____

3 What is main topic of the first paragraph? _____

_____

_____

4 How many details tell about the second main idea? _____

Use the lines on the next page to develop an outline for preparing an interesting and unusual dish that your family enjoys.

How to Prepare _____

I. Background about the dish

    A. _____

    B. _____

    C. _____

    D. _____

II. Ingredients

    A. _____

    B. _____

    C. _____

    D. _____

III. Equipment

    A. _____

    B. _____

    C. _____

    D. _____

IV. Steps

    A. _____

    B. _____

    C. _____

    D. _____

Read All About It!

A news story reports just the facts about an event and answers the questions *who, what, when, where, why*, and *how*. The most important information is included at the beginning of the article in a paragraph called the **lead**.

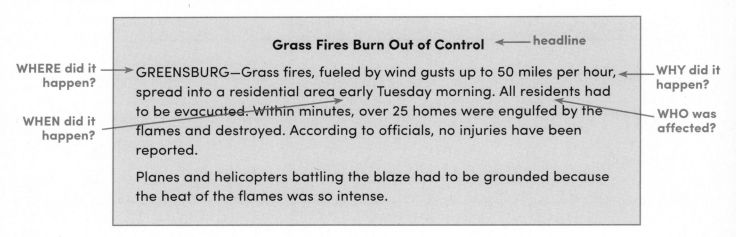

Grass Fires Burn Out of Control ← headline

WHERE did it happen? →

WHEN did it happen? →

GREENSBURG—Grass fires, fueled by wind gusts up to 50 miles per hour, spread into a residential area early Tuesday morning. All residents had to be evacuated. Within minutes, over 25 homes were engulfed by the flames and destroyed. According to officials, no injuries have been reported.

Planes and helicopters battling the blaze had to be grounded because the heat of the flames was so intense.

← WHY did it happen?

← WHO was affected?

Write a news story using the information below. Remember to write about the facts and events in the order they occurred. Follow the model lead above.

Who: Roseville Emergency Rescue Team
When: April 10, 2019; 5 A.M.
Where: Slate Run River
What: team and rescue vehicles sent; worked for three hours; rescued residents

How: used helicopter and boats
Why: residents along river stranded by flash flood after storm

_____

_____

_____

_____

_____

_____

_____

© Scholastic Inc.

ANSWER KEY

Page 5
Sentences will vary.

Page 6
Column 1: P, P, S, S, P, S
Column 2: P, P, P, S, S, S
1. The show must go on.
2. One rotten apple spoils the whole barrel.
3. Every cloud has a silver lining.
4. The early bird catches the worm.
5. A rolling stone gathers no moss.
6. Haste makes waste.

Pages 7–8
1. S **2.** E **3.** S **4.** Q **5.** C
6. E **7.** C **8.** E **9.** S **10.** Q
Sentences will vary.

Page 9
1. Did you know that the whale shark can grow to a length of 60 feet?
2. These huge creatures are not a threat to humans like some other sharks are.
3. Whale sharks float near the surface to look for plankton and tiny fish.
1. There are an estimated 32,000 known species of fish in the world.
2. Is the dwarf pygmy goby one of the smallest of all these species?
3. This species of goby is less than a half-inch long when it is fully grown!

Page 10
1. Are numbers that cannot be divided evenly by 2 called odd numbers?
2. Can all even numbers be divided evenly by 2?
3. Is zero considered an even number?
4. Are numbers that have 0, 2, 4, 6, or 8 in the ones place even numbers?
5. Do odd numbers end in 1, 3, 5, 7, or 9?
6. Is the number 317,592 an even number because it ends in 2?
7. Is the sum always an even number when you add two even numbers?

Page 11
Think about the fastest car you've ever seen in the Indianapolis 500 race. That's about how fast peregrine falcons dive. They can actually reach speeds of over 200 miles an hour while diving. How incredibly fast they are! Peregrine falcons are also very powerful birds. Did you know that they can catch and kill their prey in the air using their sharp claws? What's really amazing is that peregrine falcons live in both the country and the city. Keep on the lookout if you're ever in New York City. Believe it or not, it is home to several falcons.

Page 12
Answers will vary.

Page 13
Sentences will vary.

Page 14
Answers and sentences will vary.

Page 15
1. My sister Annie has always participated in sports, and many say she's a natural athlete.
2. Soccer, basketball, and softball are fun, but she wanted a new challenge.
3. Will Dad convince her to try skiing, or will he suggest ice skating?

Page 16
1. The Caspian Sea, the world's largest lake, covers an area about the same size as Montana.
2. The Komodo dragon, a member of the monitor family, can grow to a length of 10 feet.
3. Our closest star, the sun, is estimated to be more than 27,000,000°F at its core.

Page 17
1. My brothers built a tree house in the old oak tree in our backyard.
2. Jim made a sturdy rope ladder for the tree house.
3. Kyle bought a gallon of brown paint.
4. Kyle and Jim finished painting the walls in an hour.

Page 18
1. Before the movie was over, the power went out.
2. Jago was in his room because he had homework to do.
3. While I waited for my parents to come home, I watched a movie.

Page 19
Sentences will vary.

Page 20
1. I'd like a bike, a pair of in-line skates, and a snowboard for my birthday.
2. Well, my friend, you can't always have what you want when you want it.
3. No, but I can always hope!
4. I used to like skateboarding, but now I prefer snowboarding and ice skating.
5. What sports, games, or hobbies do you enjoy most, Jody?
6. I learned to ski last year, and now I'm taking ice-skating lessons.
Sentences will vary.

Page 21
1. While Gina answered the phone, Marta opened the front door.
2. Just as Gina said, "Hello," the caller hung up.
3. Unless they hurried, the girls were going to miss the one o'clock show.
4. By the time they got to the corner, the bus had already come and gone.
5. After the girls had waited a half hour, the next bus to town finally showed up.

Page 22
1. The United States is the top meat-eating country in the world. Each person consumes about 220 pounds of meat each year! Beef is the most commonly eaten meat.
2. Have you ever noticed that Abraham Lincoln faces right on a penny? He is not the only president on a U.S. coin who does. Thomas Jefferson faces right on newer nickels, too.
3. It would be fantastic to have a robot to do all my chores, help do my homework, and play games. I really think the day will come. Unfortunately, it won't come soon enough for me.

Page 23

Some of the words may vary.

How would **you** like to go to school on Saturdays? If you lived in the **country** of Japan, that's just where you'd be each Saturday morning. I have a **friend** who lives in Japan. Yuichi explained that **students** attend classes five and one-half **days** a week. The **half** day is on Saturday. I was also surprised to **learn** that the Japanese school **year** is one of the longest in the world—about 220 days. It begins in the **month** of April. While we have over two months off each **summer**, students in Japan get their **vacation** in late July and August. School then **begins** again in fall and ends in March. The people of **Japan** believe that a good **education** is very important. Children are required to attend school from the age of six to the **age** of fifteen. They have elementary and middle **schools** just like we do. Then most **students** go on to high **school** for another three years. Yuichi says that students work very **hard** because the standards are so high. He and some of his friends even **take** extra classes after school. They all want to get into a good **college** someday.

Page 24

Starting Over

Today started off badly and only got worse. Everyone in my family woke up late this morning. I had only 15 minutes to get ready and catch the bus. I dressed as fast as I could, grabbed an apple and my backpack, and raced to get to the bus stop on time. Fortunately, I just made it. Unfortunately, the bus was pulling away when several kids pointed out that I had on two different shoes. At that moment, I wanted to start the day over.

Page 25

Topic sentences will vary.

Page 26

Topic sentences will vary.

Page 27

Topic sentences will vary.

Page 28

Topic sentence: Tony Hawk was an extraordinary skateboarder.
Supporting sentences: He turned professional when he was only 14 years old. Now retired, Tony made history in 1999 by landing a trick called the "900" at the Summer X Games.
Closing sentence: Tony Hawk may just be the greatest skateboarder ever. Paragraphs will vary.

Page 29

Topic sentence: Yesterday our science class went on a field trip to a pond.
Unrelated supporting sentences: Next month, we're going to the ocean. That will be fun. One of the boys accidentally fell in. He was really embarrassed.

Page 30

Supporting sentences will vary.

Page 31

Paragraphs will vary.

Page 32

1. O **2.** F **3.** F **4.** O **5.** F **6.** O
Fact and opinion sentences will vary.

Page 33

Paragraphs will vary.

Page 34

Responses and paragraphs will vary.

Page 35

Responses will vary.

Page 36

1. Max had forgotten to check the pot of stew heating up on the stove.
2. Effects: the stew boiled over, the bottom of the pot was scorched, smoke filled the kitchen, dinner was ruined, Max was in big trouble
Paragraphs will vary.

Page 37

Words, phrases, and paragraphs will vary.

Page 38

Overused words in paragraph: good, nice, little, big, bad, hard, afraid, sad
Synonyms will vary.

Page 39

1. went **2.** ran **3.** blew
4. cleaned **5.** laughed
6. ate **7.** liked
Exact verbs will vary.

Page 40

Responses will vary.

Page 41

Responses will vary.

Page 42

Responses will vary.

Page 43

Responses will vary, but all should include commas and quotation marks around the direct words of speakers.

Pages 44–45

1. Chester Greenwood **2.** three
3. Who was Chester Greenwood?
4. four
Outlines will vary.

Page 46

Responses will vary.